Published by A & C Black (Publishers) Limited
35 Bedford Row, London WC1R 4JH

Text © 1989 Jennifer Coldrey
Photographs © 1989 George Bernard

Acknowledgements
The illustrations are by Helen Senior

A CIP catalogue record for this book is available from the British Library

ISBN 0 7136 3095 7

Filmset by August Filmsetting, Haydock, St Helens
Printed in Belgium by Henri Proost & Cie Pvba

Hyacinth

Jennifer Coldrey
Photographs by George Bernard

A & C Black · London

Here is a bulb.

Have you ever seen flowers like these?

They are called hyacinths.
They grow in parks and gardens.
Sometimes people grow them indoors in bowls.

Look at the big photograph. Each hyacinth grows from
a bulb like this one.

This book will tell you how a hyacinth grows.

The new shoot is ready to grow.

The outside of the bulb is thin, like paper. It is made of old leaves. This bulb is cut in half so you can see inside it.

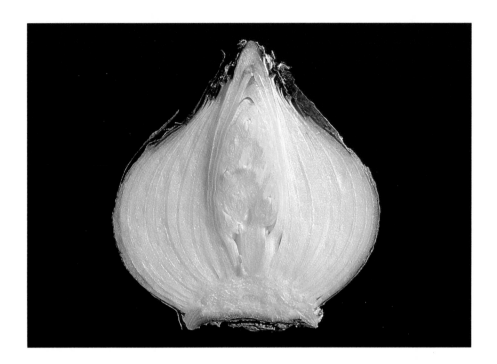

The new shoot is in the middle of the bulb. The white layers are full of food for the new shoot.

In autumn, the bulb starts to grow roots. Then in spring, a tiny shoot starts to poke through the top of the bulb.

The shoot grows bigger.

After three weeks, the shoot has grown bigger.
It still gets food from the bulb.

The plant grows more roots down into the soil.
Here is part of a root.

Can you see the tiny hairs on the root? These hairs
take in water from the soil. The plant needs water
to live and grow.

The leaves open.

As the plant gets bigger, the leaves open out. Now the leaves are tall and strong. Inside each leaf there are lots of special tubes called veins.

The leaves use sunlight to make food for the plant. The food is carried down to the plant in the veins.

Look at the big photograph. After a few weeks, flower buds begin to show between the leaves.

The flower buds start to open.

The flower stem grows longer. It pushes the flower up above the leaves.

The hyacinth flower is made of lots of little flowers. Look at the small photograph.

These flower buds are shown close-up. They are still tightly closed.

As the weather gets warmer, the buds turn pink. Then they open. Look at the big photograph. The bottom flowers open first.

Now all the flowers are open.

After about a week, all the flowers are open.
They smell very sweet.

The plant has used up nearly all the food in the bulb.
It makes its own food in the leaves.

Look at the big photograph. Each small flower is joined
to the main stem. The flower has six petals. They are
joined together at the bottom to make a tube.

Insects visit the flowers.

This flower has been cut in half.

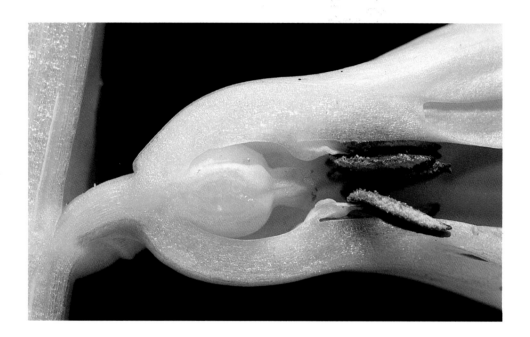

Inside the flower there are tiny stalks. They are covered with yellow dust called pollen. At the bottom of the flower, tiny seeds are waiting to grow.

On a sunny day, bees visit the flowers to look for food. Look at the big photograph. When a bee crawls inside a flower, it gets pollen on its hairy body. Can you see the yellow blob of pollen on this bee's leg?

The flowers dry up. The seeds start to grow.

When the bee visits another flower, some of the pollen may rub off. If the pollen touches the middle of this flower, tiny seeds may start to grow.

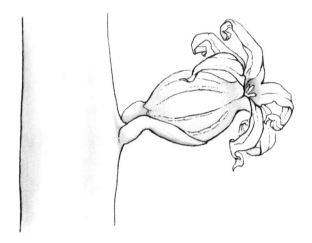

Look at the big photograph. The flowers on this hyacinth are drying up. Inside each of the flowers, seeds are growing.

The seeds grow bigger.

As the seeds grow bigger, each flower dries up and dies.

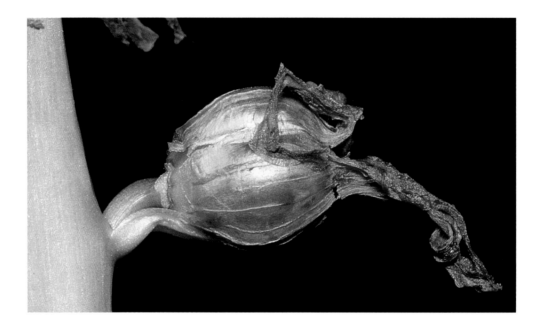

The seeds are safe inside a pod. Each pod is attached to the stem of the hyacinth.

Look at the big photograph. This seed pod has been cut in half.

Can you see three tiny seeds? Each seed has a watery middle with a white skin around it.

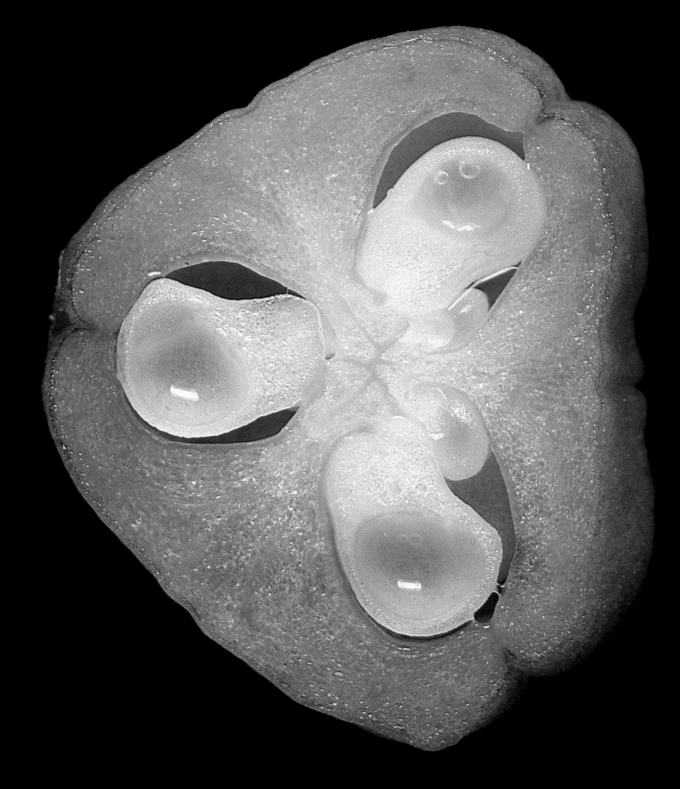

The hyacinth plant dies.

As the hyacinth dries up, its stem bends over to the ground. When the plant dies, some of the seeds may fall on to the soil. If this happens, tiny hyacinth plants may start to grow.

The leaves of the hyacinth turn yellow and dry up.

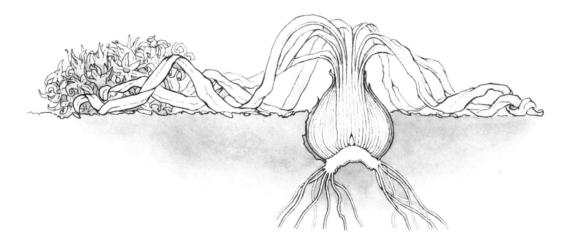

Under the ground, inside the bulb, the bottoms of the leaves do not die. They are full of food. Next year, when a new plant grows, it will use this food.

The bulb rests through the summer.

The bulb rests through the summer. The roots die.
There are no leaves above the ground.

But the bulb does not die. Inside, a new shoot is
growing.

Look at the big photograph. Next spring, a tiny shoot
appears above the soil.

What do you think will happen then?

Do you remember how a bulb grows?
See if you can tell the story in your own words.
You can use these pictures to help you.

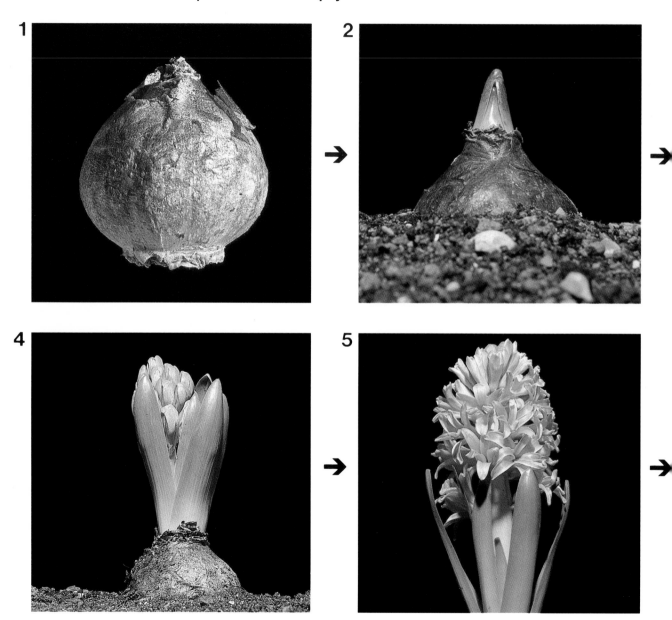

3

6

You can grow a hyacinth in a jar of water. Watch it put down roots and see the shoot grow into a flower.

Index

This index will help you to find some of the important words in the book.